T0077973

12 RULES AND 50 SUGGESTIONS FOR RAISING KIDS

Read in a short time for a lifetime of benefit

Pamela Derry

authorHOUSE®

AuthorHouse™
1663 Liberty Drive
Bloomington, IN 47403
www.authorhouse.com
Phone: 833-262-8899

Published by AuthorHouse 05/18/2022

ISBN: 978-1-6655-6017-7 (sc)
ISBN: 978-1-6655-6016-0 (e)

Print information available on the last page.

CONTENTS

INTRODUCTION

Titus 2:3 *Older women likewise are to be reverent in their behavior, not malicious gossips nor enslaved to much wine, teaching what is good, so that they may encourage the young women to love their husbands, <u>to love their children</u>, to be sensible, pure, workers at home, kind, being subject to their own husbands, so that the word of God will not be dishonored* (NASB emphasis added).

This booklet was written by an "older woman." Not a self-proclaimed expert – no PhD, just a mom who has a desire to share with families for the purpose of glorifying God.

Many verses in the Bible speak of the "rod of discipline." This author does not promote cruel beatings or the actual use of a rod – and does not believe that is the intention God had in mind. In context, that physical description appears to show the serious need for parents to effectively discipline their children.

This author also believes that God instituted corporal punishment when necessary but never out of anger. Depending on the behavior and personality of the child, standing in a corner, sitting on a chair, or taking away privileges can work effectively; Other times, a swat on the bottom might be needed.

Children are a precious gift from God.
We learn so much about God's love for us,
through the raising of our own children.

PART ONE
12 Rules

RULE #1

God is the Authority

Some people may ask, "Why doesn't God give more instructions for parenting?" Seems like a good question. However, His Word says, "Grace and peace be multiplied to you in the knowledge of God and of Jesus our Lord; seeing that His divine power has granted to us **everything** pertaining to life and godliness, through the true knowledge of Him who called us by His own glory and excellence" (2 Peter 1:2,3 emphasis added).

Eventually, children grow up and make their own choices in life. God has given a pattern to be followed so they will be equipped for sound judgment. Parents want their kids to grow up to be productive, responsible adults. The main goal, however, must be that they are heaven bound when all the temporary (physical) goes away and they step into eternity.

Acknowledgment of Rule #1 goes further to say, "God is the Ultimate Authority." There are those who profess to be an expert or an authority on raising kids. Every generation has a "new and better way" that the "experts" convince well-intended parents to follow.

With the bookshelves full of such experts, one might ask, "Why is our culture in the state that it is in with so much information available to parents today?" The further away from God's instructions, the more corrupt a society becomes, even if it seemed like a good idea at the time.

So, we begin this journey to raise our kids committed to the Ultimate Authority even if it contradicts today's "experts," how I was raised, or how I might "feel" about the matter. If God says it – that settles it.

James 1:5 *But if any of you lacks wisdom, let him ask of God, who gives to all generously and without reproach, and it will be given to him. But he must ask in faith …*

"Obey God and leave the consequences to Him."
-Dr. Charles Stanley

Reflection from Rule #1

Have you questioned how your children should be raised? Why?

Have you found yourself looking for expert advice? Where?

Have the books you read make sense to you? What was a good point?

Have you seen positive or negative results from advice in the past? Describe:

Have you found yourself following patterns from your childhood? What were they?

Do you believe that the Creator is the BEST source?

NOTES:

RULE #2

You are the PARENT –
They are the CHILDREN
don't get the two roles confused

I remember when I was about eight years old, asking, "Dad, how old do I have to be before I don't have to listen to you anymore?" His reply, "As long as you live in this house, you will obey because you HAVE to. Then when you move out, you will listen because you WANT to." At that time, (under my breath of course), I said, "That'll be the day … as soon as I'm out of here, I won't listen anymore." Because he was the parent and I was the child, it turned out as he said it would. Later in life, we became friends with a respect for the adult that we both were. When he did offer his opinion on a matter – guess what? I listened – because I wanted to.

When I was raising my kids, I was the adult, and they were the kids. There was never any doubt about that. I read my Bible, listened to older women who raised kids, asked God for wisdom, read parenting books by Dr. James Dobson, and prayed continually. Even though I made my share of mistakes, my kids had a confident PARENT. We were not each other's friend. I had my friends and they had theirs. However, now that they are grown with children of their own, we are friends.

Face it, our kids will not like it when they don't get their own way. Who does? We don't need to fix it so they will be our friend. We are the adult (the parent) and they are the children.

This might be a good time to check our own anxiety level and evaluate how we have positioned ourselves. If we are unsure of our role as a parent, the kids will pick up on that and USE IT AGAINST US. They can read our emotions. This might be a good self-check:

Why am I anxious right now? Johnny is 6 years old and I am 30 –
Why would any 30-year-old get anxious about anything that a 6-year-old would do?

We can relax and do what we need to do to take care of the situation. Parents need to get this settled in their minds. We are the person in authority NOT the child. Johnny has only had six Christmases.

Kids NEED a Confident Parent!

Reflection from Rule #2

Are you confident as a parent?

When do you seem to struggle?

Do you believe it is important for kids to have a confident parent?

Why?

What do you need to do to improve your confidence?

NOTES:

RULE #3

Children are Foolish

"Foolishness is bound up in the heart of a child; The rod of discipline will remove it far from him," (Proverbs 22:15). The definition of foolish from this Hebrew text is *stupid one or to become stupid.*

Does this say, "Only some children have foolishness?" The state of all children is foolishness. We don't like to use the word "stupid" and should never call our children "stupid" – God says children are foolish in their thinking. Their thought process is stupid.

A five-year-old is capable of memorizing and quoting Chapters from the Bible. That same five-year-old can throw himself on the floor at the grocery store because he didn't get the candy at the checkout. As far as his foolish five-year-old mind knows, this is the worst thing in the world.

Are Attention Deficit Disorders and Defiance Disorders the result of the foolishness that is bound up in the heart of the child that God says needs to be trained out of them? Is God wrong and the medical and pharmaceutical communities right and all they really need is a pill?

According to the Ultimate Authority – what removes the foolishness?

The Bible has much to say about wise and foolish men. Below is a list of verses that are applicable to our study:

- A wise son makes a father glad, but a foolish son is a grief to his mother (Proverbs 10:1)
- A wise son makes a father glad, but a foolish man despises his mother (Proverbs 15:20)
- A foolish son is a grief to his father and bitterness to her who bore him (Proverbs 17:25)
- The foolishness of man ruins his way, and his heart rages against the Lord (Proverbs 19:3)

If we want to gain more confidence in our decisions for discipline, we should look up other Scriptures about fools and foolishness and see how God compares it to wisdom and life.

Prepare for Wisdom

Reflection from Rule #3

How would you describe "foolishness"?

What are some examples of foolishness that you have seen in your child?

Since God said foolishness is bound up in a child, do you think they have the capability of recognizing it or do they need help?

What did God say gets rid of the foolishness?

Have you seen adults who still have foolish behaviors? What were they?

What did you understand from the Bibles comparisons of foolishness and wisdom?

NOTES:

RULE #4

Discipline is Love

He who withholds his rod hates his son, but he who loves him disciplines him diligently (Proverbs 13:24).

Furthermore, we had earthly fathers to discipline us, and we respected them; shall we not much rather be subject to the Father of spirits, and live? For they disciplined us for a short time as seemed best to them, but He disciplines us for our good, so that we may share His holiness. All discipline for the moment seems not to be joyful, but sorrowful; yet to those who have been trained by it, afterwards it yields the peaceful fruit of righteousness (Hebrews 12:9-11).

There is so much information in these verses!

Which parent hates his child?

Which parent loves his child?

How does today's culture contradict what God says?

Which one do you lean toward?

Parents are to discipline "diligently." Not when he/she (the parent) is in a bad mood. Not when people are watching. Not when the parent has told the child three times and now, she is going to do something about it. Not when the parent has the time, etc.

It is interesting to read in this Hebrews verse that parents discipline "as it seems best to them." This should be encouraging to all parents. God certainly knows that we will not and do not always have all the answers, but He trusts us to do what "seems best" at the time. Then that same verse goes on to say that those who are trained by discipline yield "the peaceful fruit of righteousness."

We can also see that the purpose in this verse is to train a child. Children need guidance from parents who will not use excuses for why their child behaves in a negative manner.

The key is – stay diligent – keep working on it.
We are the PARENT. They are the CHILDREN.
They need us to love them enough to train them for life.

Reflection from Rule #4

Who loves the child?

Who hates the child?

What action does a parent take when they love their child?

How often?

What do you think God means when he says the parent who does not discipline diligently – hates his child?

Are you diligent?

When are you the most tempted to NOT be diligent?

What can you do to change?

NOTES:

RULE #5

Do Not Provoke to Anger

Fathers do not provoke your children to anger but bring them up in the discipline and instruction of the Lord (Ephesians 6:4).

- Provoke children to anger by being inconsistent
- Provoke children to anger when a parent disciplines out of his/her own anger or for selfish agendas
- Provoke children when you discipline because you have had a bad day
- Provoke children by showing favoritism
- Provoke children to anger when you compare them to other people in a negative way
- Provoke children by expecting them to fulfill your own dreams
- Provoke children to anger by showing them more discipline than you show love and approval

God is Love! God is Consistent! God is Always there for Us!

...My son, do not regard lightly the discipline of the Lord, ... for those whom He loves He disciplines ... (Hebrews 12:5, 6 NASB)

It might be that the parents' image of God (as Father), could have an impact on how they discipline their own children. Perhaps, it would be helpful to evaluate our image of God to see if that is the TRUE God.

- Is our image of God as one who leaves us if we don't meet His expectations? If so, where did this image come from?
- Is our image of God as one who loves us today because we were "good" but if we don't do exactly as He says, He turns His back on us? Where did we get this image?
- Is God out there somewhere in the distant? Where did this come from?
- Is God the one who doesn't have time for us? Who taught this?
- Have we bought into the view that God is so loving that He would never discipline?
- Do we believe God would never punish anyone?

The TRUE Father God loves us and will not leave His children!
The TRUE God wants us to have peace and life!
Because the TRUE God loves us, He disciplines when it is needed.

Reflection from Rule #5

Have you done anything to provoke your child to anger?
Write it down:

Why do you think this happened?

What can you do to correct it?

NOTES:

RULE #6

Children – Obey the Parents

Children obey your parents in the Lord, for this is right. Honor your Father and Mother (which is the first commandment with a promise). So that it may be well with you, and that you may live long on the earth (Ephesians 6:1-3)

It is interesting that this commandment (Honor your Father and Mother), is among the Ten Commandments. It sits right alongside, "Thou Shall Not Murder." From God's perspective, each holds equal value and seriousness. James 2:11 says, *For He who said, "Do not commit adultery," also said, "Do not commit murder." Now if you do not commit adultery, but do commit murder, you have become a transgressor of the law.*

Obedience is never an option for a child. Children should not have the choice of whether they will obey or disobey. (Remember, the foolishness of the child – thinking that not getting the candy is the end of his/her world). Parents should not make excuses for a child's negative behavior or give themselves their own excuses for not correcting a disobedient child.

God tells us why: "So it will go well with them." (Review from Hebrews 12:9-11)

God gave children the command to HONOR parents.

This might be a good time to self-examine: Do we feel worthy of honor? God has blessed us with these children and has trusted us to raise them for Him. The picture we have of ourselves might interfere with our ability to carry out our responsibilities as a parent. When we really think about it, none of us are good enough to be what we would consider "a perfect parent".

I know many people who have never had kids think that they would be the perfect parent, but we all know how that changes when little Johnny turns age two.

Raising kids helps us better understand God's love for us. Amazingly, God Almighty loves us – with all our inadequacies. He disciplines us along the way so we can live a productive life.

**He teaches us how to honor Him by teaching us to obey so,
"It will go well with us."**

Reflections from Rule #6

Have you been diligent to be certain your child obeys?

Have you made it difficult for your child to obey?

What are some events or reasons your child did not obey?

Have you been disappointed in your reaction and then tried to make up for it by allowing the child to be disobedient?

When:

Is your child responsible for your actions or reactions?

Do you need to seek some counsel?

NOTES:

RULE #7

Good Attitude is a Must

The Bible tells us the story of Cain and Abel and how Abel had a good attitude and Cain did not. *Then the Lord said to Cain, "Why are you angry? And why has your countenance fallen? If you do well, will not your countenance be lifted up? And if you do not do well, sin is crouching at the door, and its desire is for you, but you must master it (Genesis 4:6, 7).*

The dictionary's definition of countenance: *the appearance, especially the look or expression of the face.*

A child needs to learn about attitude. While he may express disappointment, self-discipline should be taught as he manages the expression of his face (his countenance). He must master it. He may not clinch his teeth in anger any more than he should be permitted to slam the bedroom door. He must master it. Why? Because sin is crouching at the door and its desire is for him.

Cain did not obey the Lord and as a result he killed his brother. I wonder how many people in prison today stomped away in anger at the age of four and that anger continued to escalate at age eight … ten … and then into adulthood (sin was crouching at his door). How many people have lost their job because of an angry countenance? How many marriages have failed?

PARENTS *"You must master it!"* **TOO! Fix your own countenance!**

The old saying, "Do as I say, not as I do," is nowhere to be found in the Bible. This saying is an excuse passed down through the generations for poor adult behavior. "You must master it." Sin is crouching at your door and its desire is for you and your family.

We are the adults, the parent, the example, the mentor – we are all grown up. Parents need to have appropriate, mature adult actions.

This is no small matter!
Sin is crouching at your door –
And its desire is for our families.

DECIDE IT! — FIX IT! — TEACH IT! — BREAK THE CYCLE!

Reflection from Rule #7

Do you believe attitude is important?

How has your attitude been when things don't go the way you would like?

How do you respond?

How has your example been?

When do you find it the hardest to have a good attitude?

Is there something you can do to make it better?

Could a family work on attitudes together?

NOTES:

RULE #8

Step into the Future

How many times, do we as parents, just want to give in? Yes, we grounded them for one week but after all, they have been good now for three days and this is an unexpected special event that just came up. Perhaps, I could just "unground" them today and then "ground" them tomorrow to finish up the sentencing.

Look to the future: If they get expelled from school for three days, will they be able to return after one day for the special guest speaker? When they get a traffic ticket will they only need to pay half of it because they have a car payment? If there is a jail sentence for thirty days, will they get out on the twenty-ninth day for the family reunion?

Be careful of the punishment. If we take away privileges, we might start with lesser length of time so we can stick with it – perhaps a one- or two-day restriction would have been enough. We can always go up (if needed).

Step into the future: You just witnessed Susie taking her little brother's toy, but he didn't cry, so is that okay? Or maybe, you noticed little Johnny tucked another child's toy in his pocket to take home. Is it alright because you caught him before he walked out the door?

When we are the most tempted to look the other way, the question should be, "If this behavior continues what will my child look like when he is ten – a teenager – a young adult – or has his own children?" When we look ahead to the future, perhaps we will not want to just "let it go."

There is nothing wrong with occasional grace. After all, God is merciful and full of grace. However, it is too confusing to a child if this grace is seen as dad or mom not meaning what they say.

Most importantly, if negative behavior is not corrected – will they be able to be obedient to God (since parents are the first example of authority). And then – where will they spend eternity?

Proverbs 14:12 *There is a way which seems right to a man, but its end is the way of death.*

Look to the Future
Give them the tools for life eternal in Heaven!

Reflection from Rule #8

List any behavior you see in your child that needs to be improved so he/she can be a productive adult, living life to his/her fullest potential in God?

Name: Behavior:

If not corrected, what might some consequence be when he/she is 21?

If not corrected, what would that look like when married?

Change doesn't happen overnight – What are some steps you might do to help?

Name: Behavior:

If not corrected, what might some consequence be when he/she is 21?

If not corrected, what would that look like when married?

Change doesn't happen overnight – What are some steps you might do to help?

NOTES:

RULE #9

Track Your Progress

The Hebrews 12 passage taught us "For they [parents] disciplined us for a **short time** as seemed best to them..." A parent gets eighteen years (a short time – 216 months) to take a child from total dependence on you to total independence. A short time to help the child learn responsibility, self-discipline, honesty, etc.

Far too often, children in our culture are given too much responsibility at a very young age. There are kids forced into the role of parent. Eight-year-olds taking care of younger siblings because there is no responsible parent, never experience just being kids.

The flip side, however, are the parents who hold on too long and do too much. These kids are thrown out in the world and clueless about how to take care of personal needs or how to make responsible decisions. Eighteen-year-olds who are still living in foolishness is not a good place for them to be.

Along the way, a five or six-year-old can learn how to put his own clothes away, and maybe make his own sandwich and remember to get his own homework done and a permission slip signed. A four-year old can pick up his toys, help feed the dog, and hang his coat on the hook by the door.

Can the thirteen-year-old have a designated day to do his own laundry – wash it, fold it, and put it away? Perhaps he/she could prepare a family meal once a week or cut the grass weekly without being told.

Would it be important for a child to have daily personal responsibilities that begins at a very young age? Should that responsibility increase as the child matures so they are ready for the world?

By the time a child is sixteen years old they should be at a place to be trusted and self-sufficient. If not, they have no business with a driver's license. After sixteen, we have two more years (24 months) to monitor their choices and guide them while we still have legal authority. If we wait to see what choices they will make at eighteen, we will have no rights over their choices.

At age eight or nine they are halfway to having the legal right to make their own decisions. We have 96-108 months. How are we preparing them?

**Our job is to work ourselves out of the
job – we only have a short time!**

Reflection from Rule #9

List your children's name. Then calculate how many months are left until he is 16. Write things that might be improved.

Name: _____   Months until 16: _____

Improvements that need made:

How can I make those improvements?

Name: Months until 16:

Improvements that need made:

How can I make those improvements?

Name: Months until 16:

Improvements that need made:

How can I make those improvements?

NOTES:

RULE #10

Don't Allow the Blame Game

Have you noticed that today's culture has promoted the "Blame Game"? There are a multitude of excuses and ways to blame others or circumstances. We must make things "fair" we are told. Everyone gets the trophy even if they didn't do anything to contribute – they get it because they showed up. Three strikes and you're out – so people don't change their behavior until they are on their way to the third strike or they blame the boss because they lost their job – after all, they really were sick this time.

When my daughter was sixteen, our family moved to an affluent area in the suburbs. I made my kids work for their cars. My daughter drove her used Buick Skylark to school. She came home one day and said, "It's not fair, the kids at school are driving new nice cars that their parents pay for – some of them are Mercedes or BMW's and here I am driving a ten-year-old car that I have to work for."

My Response:

- Get over it! Life is not always fair. What is fair when there are starving children and we throw food away?
- Yesterday, when I drove by school, I noticed there were about fifteen buses lined up in that parking lot – each one of them full of students. So, since it's not fair that you get to drive a car, maybe you should get on the bus.

Modern philosophy states that parents should always make it fair. Well — how's that working out for us?

NO BLAMING SOMEONE ELSE.

"You made me mad!" No one MAKES another person mad. Each person choses how he/she will respond to circumstances in life.

Ezekiel 18:20 *The person who sins will die. The son will not bear the punishment for the father's iniquity, nor will the father bear the punishment for the son's iniquity ...*

Romans 14:12 *each one of us will give an account of himself to God.*

Parents need to take responsibility for their actions and not blame the kids or circumstances.

Kids need to be acknowledged for their own successes and pay consequences for their own actions without blaming others or circumstances.

Reflection Rule #10

Have you blamed your children for any negative responses?

What were the circumstances?

When you take an honest look at your reaction, what was the real reason for your negative response?

How did your parents respond when you were a child?

Do you see any similarities?

Have you seen situations when you permitted others to blame you for their own actions or reactions?

Train your mind to take the time to evaluate WHY you act or react to situations.

NOTES:

RULE #11

No Pity Party or Continuing Guilt

It is amazing to see how smart (manipulative) children can be. To think that a six-year-old can produce real tears and say, "You don't love me anymore" while at the same time, watching to see our reaction is truly amazing. And guess what? – it works quite well if we have made mistakes and never dealt with our own guilt.

Parents are new to parenting – we are just learning along the way – we will make mistakes!

Proverbs 23:7 *For as he [a person] thinks within himself, so he is.* No pity party – we don't think or say, "I'm such a terrible parent." Instead, "I love my kids and am so thankful for them – most of the time I make good decisions that keeps them cared for and safe. Sometimes, I fall short of the parent I want to be, but I learn and grow from those mistakes."

If necessary, we can apologize to children with these things in mind:

- We should not give an excuse for our behavior – like, we had a bad day at work, or we weren't feeling good. And we should **never blame them**! "I lost my temper because I just had it with you."
- It is enough to say, "I am sorry for getting angry yesterday, I should not have reacted that way," **(end of conversation)**.
- I think it's a mistake to ask for their forgiveness – doing so, puts the child in the authority position.

- These apologies should be <u>limited</u> to just a couple in a child's lifetime – even though we will certainly make more than two. Children need to have confidence in us, our authority, and our decisions.
- We can take **all** our mistakes to God in prayer – not to the kids. We ask God to help us learn more about ourselves and our reactions. We can talk with our spouse or get godly counsel if we continue acting out in a negative way.

Children are new to life – they are just learning.

Even though we are all grown up now – we are learning too.

That's life – a lifetime of learning and growing!

Proverbs 23:7 *For as he [a person] thinks within himself, so he is.* Children are NOT bad. They may feel guilty for a moment but should not be left to see themselves as failures. The same goes for the parents.

The family is a wonderful unit instituted by God Almighty! Each person in the family is wonderfully created in the image of God. Family is the loving, safe place for everyone to grow!

As a family sees themselves – so they are.

Reflection from Rule #11

Do you have guilt from past circumstances?

Do you have someone you need to ask forgiveness from (other than children)?

From your viewpoint - what makes a good parent?

From your list, which qualities do you have?

Which one(s) would like to improve?

How will you accomplish that?

Ask God for wisdom.

NOTES:

RULE #12

Love Never Fails

I Corinthians 13:1-3 *If I speak with the tongues of men and of angels, but do not have love, I have become a noisy gong or a clanging cymbal. If I have the gift of prophecy and know all mysteries and all knowledge; and if I have all faith, so as to remove mountains, but do not have love, I am nothing. And if I give all my possessions to feed the poor, and if I surrender my body to be burned, but do not have love, it profits me nothing.*

I Corinthians 13:4-8 *Love is patient, love is kind and is not jealous; love does not brag and is not arrogant, does not act unbecomingly; it does not seek its own, is not provoked, does not take into account a wrong suffered, does not rejoice in unrighteousness, but rejoices with the truth; bears all things, believes all things, hopes all things, endures all things. Love never fails; ...*

Perhaps we could take these words and apply them to parenting to make application today:

- If we have given our kids all the material things possible, or if we do all the discipline according to rules and regulations, yet we don't have (or show) love, we have become a dictator that makes a lot of noise.
- The overflow of love is patience and kindness – not seeking our own selfishness. This love does not keep a tally on all the wrongs a child may have done. Instead, this love believes that the child

is a wonderful creation of God, and God will honor our heart to raise the children in His ways.

- Love never fails. Eventually, our responsibility to discipline will be done away with, but our love will endure forever.

I Corinthians 16:13, 14 *Be on the alert, stand firm in the faith, act like men, be strong. Let all that you do be done in love.*

We need to stay strong (even when we are tired and just want to give in or give up). We are to stay on the alert – knowing there is a war for the minds of our children.

**Stand Strong in Faith
Everything we do, shall be done in love!**

Reflection from Rule #12

Write down I Corinthians 13:4-8

Instead of "trying harder" to improve on any of these, see how the Core of JESUS is LOVE and how the overflow of His Love demonstrates these characteristics. Write these down:

Whenever you might see yourself fall short of these qualities – focus on Jesus and allow what you see in Him transform you.

NOTES:

ENCOURAGEMENT

Romans 8:28 *And we know that God causes all things to work together for good to those who love God, to those who are called according to His purpose.*

Self-talk: I know that even my mistakes can be turned around for good as I learn from them, because I love God and I believe my purpose, as a parent, is to raise these precious children for Him.

PART TWO

Introduction to 50 Suggestions

Now that the twelve rules have been covered, we will review some opinions and suggestions. There is a saying, "Eat the corn and throw the cob away." Take from this list what might be helpful or maybe it will prompt you to be creative and find what fits your family's needs.

Instructions from God's Word are absolute. If suggestions match up with God's Word, then they should be considered seriously. If suggestions contradict God's Word – they should be disregarded totally. Then there are suggestions that are a matter of opinion – neither right nor wrong but may be helpful.

Here are some opinions or suggestions from a mom who has raised four kids and made plenty mistakes. I have also encouraged and coached numerous kids and families over the past twenty + years and still learning.

I am not a so called "expert" – have no PhD. I acknowledge that there is only ONE true Expert and Ultimate Authority and God alone may make that claim.

These thoughts are just from a Christian Mom who has a desire to share with families for the purpose of glorifying God.

Suggestions One through Five

1. If a child is old enough to say, "No" to his parents (out of disobedience), that child is old enough to know he should not say it again. There may be a second time but there should NOT be a third.

2. A child should not be permitted to run away from a parent. He might run once – and try it the second time but there should never be a third.

3. A child should be obedient the first time he/she is told.

4. Parents should not count: 1, 2, 2 ½ (I'm almost to 3, you better listen).

5. Parents should not bribe a child so he will obey, "If you stop crying, I'll get you some ice cream."

One through Five Notes:

Which of these did you find interesting?

What benefit (if any) do you think these suggestions might have?

Did any of these five give you some ideas that might be helpful for your family?

NOTES:

Suggestions Six through Ten

6. Parents should not threaten to use discipline – just do it! Never – "If you do that again …"

7. Parents should not threaten to leave a child. Kids need the security of their parents and to know that they will always be there.

8. Parents should not threaten to turn the child into the police. "You see that police officer over there – you'd better be good, or he will take you to jail."

9. Parents can help kids with their thoughts – example: When you stand Susie in the corner, she should say, "I'm standing in the corner because I made the choice of hitting my brother." If this is not said, Susie will have her own interpretation: "Mom is mean and that's why I'm in the corner." OR "This is my brother's fault for telling on me." Susie cannot learn personal accountability if she is permitted to blame you or her brother, even if she just thinks it. When she gets out of the corner: "Now go tell your brother you are sorry, and I trust you will make better choices so you can see the good person God created you to be." If you hear Susie say to her brother, "See what you did, you got me in trouble." IMMEDIATELY, she needs to go back in the corner to start the process again.

10. Parents should mean what they say and follow through. Think about your words. Be careful with your words. Don't make idle threats. Once it is said, you must follow through. It is not fair to children when sometimes you mean it and other times you don't.

Six through Ten Notes:

Which of these did you find interesting?

What benefit (if any) do you think these suggestions might have?

Did any of these five give you some ideas that might be helpful for your family?

Suggestions Eleven through Fifteen

11. It is good parenting to peek to make sure the child is obeying your instructions. There's nothing wrong with children thinking you have eyes in the back of your head or that you somehow can see through walls. To allow a child to think he got away with something because he was sneaky is harmful. Character is built by doing what is right when no one is looking.

12. Table manners are important tools to teach self-discipline and respect for others. Chew with your mouth closed, please pass the potatoes, take your time eating, the proper use of utensils (not fingers), and wait for everyone to finish eating before asking to be excused from the table. Dinner time can be great family time. It's a great time to discuss the day. Turn off the TV and all the noise and enjoy dinner together.

13. Most children are not hard of hearing. Instead, they are hard of listening – selectively. Don't raise your voice. Have you noticed that kids can be preoccupied with playing and you whisper to your spouse, "Would you like to go get some ice cream?" and the kids jump up and say, "Yay, ice cream." That same child, however, did not hear you say in a normal voice (not even a whispering voice), "It's time to pick up your toys." There is no need to say it louder and louder or scream. They should be trained to listen in the normal voice – the first time.

14. A parent might say, "Little Johnny just won't stand in the corner when I put him there." **W H A T ?** A six-year-old is more powerful than any adult? My son was taller and much larger than me by the time he was in the seventh grade, (I was 5'2, 120 pounds). This son was

a strong- willed child. Because he knew who was in control when he was two – that never changed when he was seventeen years old (6'3, 200 pounds).

15. Parents would be wise to understand that if a child has control at age four, it will be a disaster when he is fourteen.

Eleven through Fifteen Notes:

Which of these did you find interesting?

What benefit (if any) do you think these suggestions could have?

Did any of these five give you some ideas that might be helpful to your family?

Suggestions Sixteen
through Twenty

16. Children need to hear some praise – but overuse of praise becomes unimportant. Parents might consider reminding their children how important they are to God and how God has a special purpose for their lives.

17. Children don't need praised for doing what they should be doing anyway. Example: They don't need praised for being obedient – that is what you expected. They don't need praised for being honest – that is what is expected. They don't need praised for being nice to the sister – that is expected behavior.

18. Expect good behavior and they will see that as praise enough and no words need to be said.

19. Parents should never speak negative of their children to others if there is any chance of the kids overhearing. Remember the ice cream ears.

20. It is good for children to occasionally eavesdrop on parents telling friends about how well the child is developing in character. Example: "I saw Johnny helping Susie after she fell down and comforting her. His display of kindness and compassion made me so proud." For your child to overhear you telling another adult, is far better than your praising him directly. Again, don't overdo it! PLEASE be sure your praise is of the child's character. Be careful about praising for their performance unless you say, "Your hard work at practice paid off at

the game tonight." OR "I saw you working on your homework and it paid off – look at your grade card!" The character that produced the performance is what you are seeking.

Sixteen through Twenty Notes

Which of these did you find interesting?

What benefit (if any) do you think these suggestions could have?

Did any of these five give you some ideas that might be helpful for your family?

NOTES:

Suggestions Twenty-one through Twenty-five

21. Parents should never, never call their children negative names. Kids will become what you tell them they are. If you say, "He is so slow" – He will become even slower and that picture will follow him into his adult life. "Get your lazy butt off the couch" is destructive – provokes to anger – creates a negative image in his mind – and does NOT move a child to better behavior.

22. Children should never be compared to other children or other people. If there is a person known to your family who is considered the "black sheep" and you say, "You better be careful, or you will turn out just like Albert." Now the child sees his own image acting like Albert. Another picture that is not easily erased.

23. Children are not bad children. Nothing negative should identify them. Children are created in the image of God. They make wrong choices but so do adults. Children are trained to not call other children names – so why would the adults think it is alright to do so.

24. Your kids need to know that you love them and assure them that you know they will make a better choice the next time.

25. Don't overdo affection or praise to "make up" for exercising discipline. If that is the only time he gets praised, he will soon figure out that negative behavior gets him the attention from you that he craves.

Twenty-one through Twenty-five NOTES

Which of these did you find interesting?

What benefit (if any) do you think these suggestions could have?

Did any of these five give you some ideas that might be helpful for your family?

NOTES

Suggestions Twenty-six
through Thirty

26. One child should not be favored over another. Believe me, they know it – no matter how hard you try to not let it show! If you are struggling with this, get some help to see why this is happening. I have known of several adults who lived in homes where this was happening. Often, it was the favored child that had more challenges in life as she cannot understand why the world is not evolving around her. The less favored child tends to become the one that sticks by mom/dad throughout the adult years, as he/she continues to search for the parent's approval that the sister always had.

27. Kids don't need to be instructed in all things. Even a five-year-old knows that putting his foot out to deliberately trip his sister is not good to do. That five-year-old needs to be discipline for that – not instructed, he already knew that it was wrong.

28. As much as is possible, make the punishment or discipline relatable to the wrongdoing. Example: If a child deliberately breaks another child's toy, make the child pay with one of the toys that is special to him. Example: If the child was told to clean his room and he chooses to sit and play instead, allow him to clean it when the rest of the family is doing something fun or when his favorite special movie is on – or company comes over. Don't threaten him – don't tell him beforehand that is what is going to happen – just do it! Example: If the child is supposed to brush his teeth before bed and he plays with the toothbrush (you watch him without him knowing). You could allow

him to go to sleep and then wake him up, "Since you chose to not brush your teeth before you went to bed, you can do it now." Or if you have an extra toothbrush, you could say, "Since you decided to not use the toothbrush on your teeth, you can use it to clean the baseboards in the living room." Be sure you make the discipline age appropriate.

29. Do NOT punish the child for accidents. Do NOT react in a negative way. It is a simply spilled milk – not the end of the world. Spilled milk at the dinner table is disruptive but is normal. Show the child the best place to sit the drink and if it gets spilled remind him of the best place. If the child is running through the house and knocks over the plant – ask him if that would have happened if he were not running in the house. If the child is old enough – even though it is an accident, he can clean up the mess. "Accidents do happen, now let's go get the broom and get it cleaned up." A younger child will need your help. The older one can clean up his own mess – not as punishment, but to show that when you are not careful, it causes a mess that you need to clean. This is a physical lesson – When we create a mess in our life – we may be forgiven, but the mess will still need to be cleaned up. Remember, you are teaching what will be carried over in adult life. If you clean up what they created (accident or not) – what does that teach them?

30. When a child is excited to share with you the grade card showing a B in Math, this is not the time to talk about what needs to happen for it to be an A. Nor is it the time to say, "Well that's nice but look at this C in English." Children have such a desire to please you. If he/she sees you are pleased with the accomplishment, that will be great incentive to get the English grade to a B.

Twenty-six through Thirty Notes

Which of these did you find interesting?

What benefit (if any) do you think these suggestions could have?

Did any of these give you some ideas that might be helpful for your family?

NOTES:

Suggestions Thirty-one through Thirty-five

31. Children should never be permitted to use parents against one another. If one parent says "No," they should not be permitted to ask the other parent. If a child doesn't like the "No" he got from dad and then goes to mom for a "Yes," this might be a good time for grounding from the activity that was requested. The parent, on the other hand, should not shift responsibility to the other parent. If one is unsure of what the answer should be, don't say, "Go ask your father." The better answer would be, "I will discuss this with your father, and we will make a decision."

32. Use your "no's" responsibly. Overuse of "no" can eventually cause the parent to not mean it and not follow through. When we get in a habit of saying, "No" the child learns the process of bargaining or begging to get it changed to a "Yes". This habit is hard to break – so be careful with your answer to begin with. If needed, you can always respond by saying, "I'll think about it." If he/she continues to beg or bargain, tell him "Now the answer is "No."

33. Do not allow children to interrupt the parent who is talking. Teach them how to stand quietly and wait. Then do the same thing when they are talking with you. Don't allow another child to talk over or interrupt a sibling.

34. When possible, give them timeframes. Example: You may finish playing for ten more minutes and then you will clean up. A timer is a good thing to use to teach even the younger child what ten minutes mean. This timer is also a good tool to use when he/she needs to stand in the corner. I had a mom tell me one time that the child would reset the timer as soon as she walked out of the room. That seems like a good time to double the minutes.

35. Outburst of anger examples: #1 The child has his teeth clinched and his attitude needs adjusted. Put a mirror on the wall and have him stand there looking at his face. Tell him, "This face (countenance) must be fixed, so you stand there looking at it for the next five minutes to see how you can fix it." If it isn't fixed after the five minutes – keep setting the timer for another five minutes. Do this as many times as it takes to get the result that is needed. Several timeframes of 5 minutes are far better than a longer length of time. #2 Little Susie didn't get her way, so she stomps to her room and slams the door. In a calm voice, you respond, "Obviously you have not had enough practice on how to correctly open and close doors. So, you will now practice it. You are to go in your room, close the door correctly, open the door, walk outside the door, close the door, walk through the living room. Then walk back to your room, open the door again, close the door, and repeat the same process. Each time you walk into the living room, you count so I can hear you. 1, then 2, then 3 until you get to 10. If at any time, she shuts it with force, you say, "Oh, I see you still need more practice, so start again 1, … SPECIAL NOTE: The child will most likely get to that final 10 and she is going to close the door for the last time as she enters her room. She will give it just a tiny little nudge – just enough to show her disproval but slight enough that she can pretend it was nothing. She knows exactly what she has done. "Susie, you almost had it, but it isn't quite there yet, start again, "1."

Thirty-one through Thirty-five Notes

Which of these did you find interesting?

What benefits (if any) do you think these suggestions could have?

Did any of these give you some ideas that might be helpful for your family?

NOTES:

Suggestions Thirty-six
through Forty

36. Exercise the smallest amount of punishment to begin with. You want to have room to extend the time or consequences if needed. If you say, "You are grounded for a month," first, can you stick with it? Second, the child may give up because he/she sees no end in sight so why should she even try? Ten minutes in a corner is a long time for a six-year old and five minutes is an eternity for a three-year-old. When a child talks back or displays willful defiance one swat on the bottom may be enough but might require two swats if he turns around and sticks his tongue out at you after the first. A gradual increase, with time in between for both the parent and the child might be the most effective.

37. Don't send a child to the bedroom for punishment. The bedroom should be the place for sleeping or playing. Don't allow a child to kick and scream behind closed doors. It is inappropriate regardless.

38. Never say anything negative about the other parent to the child. If you and your spouse have a disagreement about what should be done with the children, talk it out behind closed doors. If you are unable to come to an agreement get some godly counsel. The kids need to know you are united. If one parent is harsh and the one is trying to make up for it by being too lenient, PLEASE, get some help!

39. Never say anything negative about the child's teacher, or people in authority, or the church, or the sermon when there is any possibility of

the child hearing (remember the ice cream ears). If you are questioning the teacher – go to him/her in person and talk it out.

40. Teach a child early on to say, "Please" and "Thank you." As soon as a child is old enough to ask for a drink, he is old enough to say, "Drink please." As you are handing the cookie to the child, hold on to it as he reaches for it, instruct him to "Say, thank you." Children are taught to respect by answering their parents, "Yes sir or ma'am", or "Yes Mom/Dad." It helps kids to say, Mr. Mrs. Ms. or Aunt/Uncle when addressing adults.

Thirty-six through Forty Notes

Which of these did you find interesting?

What benefit (if any) do you think these suggestions could have?

Did any of these five give you some ideas that might be helpful for your family?

Suggestions Forty-one through Forty-five

41. Take care of yourself so you can take care of the children. It is sometimes impossible to get some down time when the kids are little. Even small intervals of 10 minutes during the day or evening helps. Remember the instructions given by the flight attendants, "Secure your own mask first." This break time is for the benefit of the family – not for selfish motives. You are grown up now – life can get tough.

42. Let the kids see affection between mom and dad. When kids see mom and dad give a little kiss or a big hug, they feel secure.

43. Order is essential. Screaming and running in the house cause chaos. People talking over each other is chaos. Toys thrown all over the house and everything out of place is chaos. The TV or music blaring - chaos. Be careful though, extreme, excessive order does not promote a safe, relaxing environment for the family to enjoy.

44. When you notice a child acting out, it may be because he/she needs some extra attention. This seems to happen when you are having a busy day with so much to do. You will save yourself time and anxiety if you will just stop what you are doing and sit quietly to read the child a short book with him/her sitting close by you with lots of hugs. That little "time out" will be helpful for the rest of the day.

45. Listen intently when your child wants to talk with you about something. Show them excitement when they are excited. If they tell something

that is sad, affirm by saying, "That must have been very sad for you to hear." This is not the time to say, "You shouldn't feel that way." If you think that instruction would be of benefit – use a different time and a similar situation to do the instructing. When the child shares a special coloring page or a good grade, show them you are proud. Perhaps when dad gets home say to the child, "Hurry, go get your special paper you got from school today and show Dad."

Forty-One through Forty-five Notes

Which of these did you find interesting?

What benefit (if any) do you think these suggestions could have?

Did any of these give you some ideas that might be helpful for your family?

NOTES:

Suggestions Forty-Six through Fifty

46. Limit or get rid of all together, TV or screen time. Kids need to use their imaginations and need to learn how to play with one another. After a child is stimulated by handheld devices, nothing else is as fun in comparison. You can fool yourself into believing that you will monitor the TV program, but once the inappropriate commercial comes on and you realize it, the image is already in their minds. If you want to allow them to watch a movie, you watch it first and ask yourself what the movie might be promoting to the child. Be truthful with yourself about what you are allowing your children to do: Are you allowing it so you can have some down time? Are you allowing it because the other kids get to have iPads? Are you using it to stop the kids from fighting, so you don't have to take the time to discipline? Are you using it as a babysitter? Are you fully convinced that it isn't harmful? There is a children's song that says, "Be careful little eyes what you see – Be careful little ears what you hear". Perhaps a good adult song would be "Be careful parents what your child sees – be careful parents what your child hears." The greatest part of any individual is the mind. A child's mind is growing, learning, and developing. Can you risk the potential consequences that TV and other screen times offer? Once you are truthful with yourself about why the kids have the devices ask yourself, "Is it worth the price that cannot be bought back?"

47. Read to your kids. Get a kids Bible story book – read it to them every night when possible. A few minutes (5-10) that is done consistently is more valuable than 20 minutes today and nothing tomorrow.

48. Have fun with your kids. Joke around with your kids. Play games as a family. Let your kids see mom and dad having fun with one another. Laughter is glue for the family.

49. Assemble with other believers – every Sunday – No MATTER what. Let them know that they are special to God individually and as a family. You go to work every day, because work is important for this physical life. Don't just talk about how important God is, show them. Make Sunday a priority. Matthew 6:33 *Seek first His kingdom and His righteousness and all these things will be added to you.*

50. Pray for your family – be on guard! Be watchful! Know your child – so you know how to pray for them.

Forty-six through Fifty Notes

Which of these did you find interesting?

What benefits (if any) do you think these suggestions could have?

Did any of these five give you some ideas that might be helpful for your family?

Notes:

Reflection

As you reflect on the information in this small booklet, list three things that made the most impact on you.

What, if any, changes did you make?

Results:

NOTES:

Dwell on These Things

Philippians 4:8 *Finally brethren, whatever is true, whatever is honorable, whatever is right, whatever is pure, whatever is lovely, whatever is of good repute, if there is any excellence and if anything worthy of praise, dwell on these things. The things you have learned and received and heard and seen in me practice these things, and the God of peace will be with you.*

Answer these questions about your family:
What is true?
What is honorable?
What is right?
What is pure?
What is lovely?
What is of good repute?
What is excellent?
What is worthy of praise?

DWELL ON THESE THINGS

May the God of peace be with you.

*If this information has been helpful to you and
your family – give God the glory!*

We appreciate any comments:

pamelasderry@yahoo.com

Printed in the United States
by Baker & Taylor Publisher Services